ABOUT AUTHOR

Kamlesh Vishwakarma is a seasoned professional in the field of Amazon marketing, renowned for his extensive years of experience and expertise in ecommerce. As an Amazon-verified Advertising Partner, he showcases his credibility and proficiency in online advertising. Kamlesh consistently demonstrates strategic thinking abilities, adeptly crafting compelling content, managing advertising campaigns, and fostering online communities. His adeptness in harnessing the power of Amazon ads translates into tangible and impactful results.

Introduction To Drop Shipping

Drop shipping is a business model where retailers sell products to customers without holding inventory. Instead, they partner with suppliers or manufacturers who handle the inventory storage, order processing, and shipping. This approach minimizes upfront costs, making it an attractive option for entrepreneurs starting an online business.

How Drop shipping Works

1. **Setting Up a Store**
   The retailer sets up an online store (using platforms like Shopify, WooCommerce, or Amazon) to display and sell products.
2. **Partnering with Suppliers**
   The retailer partners with dropshipping suppliers who provide a catalog of products that can be listed on their store. Popular dropshipping suppliers include AliExpress, Oberlo, Spocket, and others.
3. **Customer Orders**
   when a customer places an order on the retailer's website, the order details are forwarded to the supplier.
4. **Supplier Fulfillment**
   The supplier processes the order, packages the product, and ships it directly to the customer.
5. **Profit Margin**
   The retailer earns a profit by charging the customer a higher price than the supplier's cost.

Advantages of Drop shipping

- **Low Initial Investment:** No need to buy inventory upfront.
- **Easy to Start:** With minimal requirements, you can focus on marketing and customer service.
- **Scalability:** Products can be added or removed easily, and suppliers handle logistical challenges.
- **Flexibility:** You can operate the business from anywhere with an internet connection.

Challenges of Drop shipping

- **Lower Profit Margins:** Competition often drives prices down, and suppliers may charge additional fees.
- **Lack of Control:** Quality, delivery times, and inventory levels depend on the supplier.
- **Customer Service Issues:** Since you don't handle products, resolving complaints can be complex.
- **Supplier Reliability:** Problems like out-of-stock items or late shipments can affect your reputation.

Is Drop shipping Right for You?

Drop shipping is ideal for those looking to enter e-commerce with minimal risk. It works best if you have skills in marketing, niche selection, and customer service. However, success depends on building a reliable supplier network and creating a strong brand identity.

Understand Amazon's Drop shipping Policy

Amazon permits drop shipping under specific conditions outlined in its drop shipping policy. To comply with Amazon's requirements, ensure the following:

1. **Be the Seller of Record**: You must be identified as the seller on all packing slips, invoices, external packaging, and related information. This means your business name should appear on all customer-facing materials.
2. **Remove Third-Party Identifiers**: Ensure that any materials identifying a third-party drop shipper are removed before shipping the order. This includes packing slips, invoices, and external packaging.
3. **Handle Returns and Customer Service**: You are responsible for accepting and processing customer returns and providing customer service for your products.
4. **Comply with Amazon's Policies**: Adhere to all terms of your seller agreement and other applicable Amazon policies.

Violating these guidelines can lead to account suspension or other penalties. For instance, purchasing products from another retailer and having them ship directly to customers, without identifying yourself as the seller, is prohibited.

By following these requirements, you can utilize drop shipping as a fulfillment method on Amazon while maintaining compliance with their policies.

Pros And Cons Of Amazon Drop Shipping

Amazon dropshipping can be an attractive option for entrepreneurs due to its low barrier to entry and potential for profit. However, like any business model, it comes with both advantages and disadvantages. Here's a breakdown of the **pros and cons**:

Pros of Amazon Dropshipping

1. **Low Startup Costs**

- **Minimal Investment**: Dropshipping eliminates the need to purchase inventory upfront. You only pay for the product when a customer places an order.
- **No Warehouse or Storage Fees**: Since products are shipped directly from the supplier to the customer, you don't need to worry about renting warehouse space or handling storage costs.

2. **No Need for Inventory Management**

- **Simplified Operations**: You don't have to manage or store products, reducing overhead costs and logistical challenges.
- **Flexibility**: You can offer a wide variety of products without worrying about inventory or stock levels, as the supplier manages it.

3. **Scalability**

- **Easy to Scale**: Since you're not dealing with inventory or order fulfillment directly, scaling your business becomes easier compared to traditional retail.
- **Global Reach**: You can potentially sell products globally without the need to manage international warehouses or shipping.

4. **Reduced Risk**

- **No Inventory Risk**: Since you don't buy products upfront, there's no risk of unsold inventory, which can be a common issue with traditional retail.
- **Low Financial Risk**: Without the need for upfront product investment, you can test various products with minimal financial commitment.

5. Automated Fulfillment

- **Automation Tools**: Many dropshipping platforms integrate with Amazon's marketplace and automate the order fulfillment process, saving time and effort.
- **Amazon FBA Integration**: You can combine dropshipping with Amazon's FBA service for faster shipping and Prime eligibility.

Cons of Amazon Dropshipping

1. Low Profit Margins

- **Slim Margins**: Due to the nature of dropshipping, you often rely on suppliers who sell at wholesale prices, and competition on Amazon can drive prices down. The small profit margins may not leave much room for growth unless you scale significantly.
- **Amazon Fees**: On top of supplier costs, Amazon charges various fees (referral fees, FBA fees, etc.), which can further erode profit margins.

2. Limited Control Over Product Quality and Shipping

- **Quality Assurance Challenges**: Since you're not handling the products yourself, there's a risk that your suppliers may not meet the quality standards you expect, potentially leading to customer dissatisfaction.
- **Shipping Delays**: You rely on third-party suppliers for fulfillment, which means you have less control over

shipping times and delays, affecting customer experience and satisfaction.

3. Dependency on Suppliers

- **Supplier Reliability**: Your business depends entirely on your supplier for product quality, shipping times, and stock levels. If the supplier faces issues (e.g., stock shortages, shipping delays), it directly impacts your business.
- **Lack of Customization**: Most dropshipping suppliers provide generic products, which makes it hard to differentiate your brand or offer custom products.

4. Risk of Account Suspension

- **Amazon Policy Violations**: Amazon has strict dropshipping policies. If you fail to meet their guidelines (such as having the supplier's information on the packing slip), you risk having your account suspended.
- **Customer Service Responsibility**: While Amazon handles many customer service aspects for FBA, dropshipping sellers are still responsible for customer service. Issues like returns, refunds, and disputes can lead to negative reviews or account penalties.

5. Competitive Market

- **High Competition**: Many sellers enter the dropshipping market, leading to intense competition,

especially in popular niches. This can make it difficult to stand out or maintain competitive pricing.
- **Saturation in Certain Niches**: Popular product categories like electronics or fashion are highly saturated, making it harder to find a profitable product.

6. Inventory Management Challenges

- **Stock Synchronization**: Since you're relying on a third-party supplier, there's a risk that the products you're selling could go out of stock without notice, leading to canceled orders or delayed shipments.
- **Multiple Suppliers**: If you work with multiple suppliers, managing inventory and fulfillment across different locations can be challenging.

7. Customer Expectations and Service

- **Customer Service Demands**: Dropshipping involves handling customer inquiries, complaints, returns, and refunds, even if you aren't physically managing the products. Failing to provide excellent customer service could result in negative reviews or account suspension.
- **Shipping Time Expectations**: If your suppliers are based overseas (e.g., China), shipping times can be long, and this may not meet customer expectations, especially if you're selling to Prime members who expect fast delivery.

8. Limited Branding and Control Over the Customer Experience

- **Lack of Branding**: In most dropshipping models, you don't have control over the product packaging or branding, which can make it harder to build a unique brand.
- **Generic Customer Experience**: The experience from order to delivery is controlled by your supplier, so customer service, packaging, and quality might not reflect your business's desired image.

Amazon dropshipping offers a relatively easy way to start an online business with low upfront costs and minimal risk, but it also comes with challenges like low profit margins, dependency on third-party suppliers, and high competition.

Success requires careful supplier selection, effective inventory management, strong customer service, and a focus on compliance with Amazon's policies. For those willing to navigate these challenges, dropshipping can be a profitable venture, but it may not be as hands-off as it initially appears.

Getting Started With Amazon Drop Shipping

Amazon dropshipping can be a lucrative business if done correctly. It involves selling products on Amazon without holding inventory, relying on suppliers to fulfill orders. Here's a step-by-step guide to get started:

Step 1: Understand Amazon's Drop shipping Policy

Before starting, familiarize yourself with Amazon's drop shipping policy. Key requirements include:

- You must be the seller of record on all invoices and packaging.
- Third-party information (like another retailer's branding) must not appear on orders.
- You are responsible for returns and customer service.

Failing to comply with Amazon's policies can result in account suspension.

Step 2: Set Up Your Amazon Seller Account

1. **Choose a Plan**:
   - **Individual Plan**: Suitable for selling fewer than 40 items per month.
   - **Professional Plan**: Best for high-volume sellers, costing $39.99/month.
2. **Register**: Sign up at Amazon Seller Central. Provide necessary information such as a business name, address, tax details, and payment information.

Step 3: List Products on Amazon

1. **Create Listings**: Use Amazon's listing tools to add products with optimized titles, descriptions, images, and bullet points.
2. **Follow Amazon's Guidelines**: Ensure listings meet content and image standards.
3. **Set Competitive Pricing**: Research competitors and adjust your pricing to stay competitive.

Step 4: Focus on Marketing and SEO

1. **Keywords**: Use tools like Helium 10 or Merchant Words to identify high-ranking keywords.
2. **Amazon PPC Ads**: Run pay-per-click campaigns to drive traffic.
3. **Promotions and Deals**: Offer discounts or promotions to attract customers.

Step 5: Manage Orders and Customer Service

1. **Order Fulfillment**: Ensure suppliers process and ship orders promptly.
2. **Customer Interaction**: Respond to queries and reviews professionally and timely.
3. **Returns and Refunds**: Handle returns in line with Amazon's return policies.

Step 6: Monitor Performance Metrics

Amazon tracks seller performance through metrics like Order Defect Rate (ODR), Late Shipment Rate (LSR), and Valid

Tracking Rate (VTR). Maintaining good metrics is crucial to avoid penalties or suspension.

Choose Your Niche and Products

Selecting the right niche and products is crucial for a successful Amazon drop shipping business. Here's a structured approach to guide you:

Step 3: Research Your Niche and Products

1. **Find Profitable Niches**: Use tools like Jungle Scout, Helium 10, or AMZScout to identify high-demand, low-competition products.
2. **Check for Amazon Restrictions**: Ensure the product isn't restricted or gated.
3. **Assess Profitability**: Calculate costs (product, shipping, Amazon fees) and ensure a healthy profit margin.

2. Identify Potential Niches

A niche is a specialized segment of the market catering to specific customer needs. To identify a profitable niche:

- **Assess Your Interests and Expertise:** Choosing a niche aligned with your passions can enhance your commitment and understanding of the market.

- **Research Market Demand:** Utilize tools like Google Trends to analyze the popularity and seasonality of potential niches. For instance, the car accessories market was valued at over $448 billion worldwide in 2023 and is projected to grow by a compound annual growth rate of 3.9% through 2030.
- **Evaluate Competition:** Analyze existing sellers in your chosen niche to understand the competitive landscape. Aim for niches with moderate competition to balance demand and market saturation.

3. Analyze Product Viability

Within your chosen niche:

- **Demand Consistency:** Opt for products with steady demand rather than fleeting trends.
- **Profit Margins:** Calculate potential profits by considering product costs, Amazon fees, and shipping expenses. Higher-margin products can offer better returns.
- **Shipping Considerations:** Prefer lightweight and non-fragile items to reduce shipping costs and minimize the risk of damage during transit.

4. Validate Product Ideas

Before listing products:

- **Keyword Research:** Use Amazon's search bar and tools like AMZScout to identify popular search terms related to your products. This helps in understanding

customer search behavior and optimizing your listings.
- **Competitor Analysis:** Examine top-selling products in your niche to identify gaps in the market or areas for differentiation.

5. Source Reliable Suppliers

Partnering with dependable suppliers ensures product quality and timely delivery.

- **Supplier Platforms:** Explore platforms like AliExpress, Oberlo, or local suppliers to find products that align with your niche.
- **Evaluate Supplier Performance:** Assess suppliers based on their ratings, reviews, and shipping capabilities.

6. Comply with Amazon's Policies

Adhere to Amazon's dropshipping policy, which mandates that you:

- Be the seller of record for your products.
- Identify yourself as the seller on all packing slips and invoices.
- Remove any information indicating a third-party seller before shipping.

Non-compliance can lead to account suspension.

Product Sourcing for Drop shipping

Product sourcing is a critical step in the drop shipping process. Choosing the right products and suppliers determines your business's success. Here's a detailed guide to sourcing products for your drop shipping business.

1. Finding the Right Products

- **Focus on Trends**: Use tools like Google Trends, TikTok, or Instagram to identify trending products.
- **Consider Passion Niches**: Products related to hobbies or lifestyles (e.g., fitness, pets, or gadgets) often sell well.
- **Avoid Highly Competitive Niches**: Look for products with moderate demand but low competition.
- **Lightweight and Easy to Ship**: Reduces shipping costs.
- **High-Profit Margin**: Aim for at least a 30-50% margin after fees and shipping.
- **Non-Seasonal**: Products with year-round demand offer consistent sales.
- **Problem-Solving**: Items that address a specific need tend to sell better.

2. Sourcing Platforms

a. AliExpress

- A popular platform for finding suppliers offering a wide range of products.

- Features include low-cost items, global shipping, and integrations with tools like Oberlo.

b. Spocket

- Offers access to suppliers, primarily in the US and Europe, for faster shipping times.
- Products are often of higher quality than AliExpress.

c. SaleHoo

- A directory of verified dropshipping suppliers.
- Offers research tools to identify profitable products.
- Reach out to manufacturers directly to negotiate dropshipping terms.
- Offers better pricing and control over quality.

3. Evaluate Suppliers

- **Reliability**: Ensure they can consistently fulfill orders.
- **Shipping Times**: Faster delivery enhances customer satisfaction.
- **Quality Control**: Test products by ordering samples.
- **Communication**: Suppliers should be responsive and professional.

Avoid Suppliers

- Suppliers that require large upfront fees.
- Poor communication or lack of transparency.
- Overpromised shipping times or inconsistent inventory.

4. Sourcing Insights Tools

- **Jungle Scout**: Ideal for Amazon-specific insights.
- **Helium 10**: Helps identify high-demand products.
- **Ecomhunt**: Curates trending products for dropshipping.
- **berlo**: Integrates with Shopify to automate product imports and order processing.
- **Zendrop**: Focuses on high-quality suppliers and faster shipping.
- **DSers**: An alternative to Oberlo for managing AliExpress orders.

5. Strategies for Effective Product Sourcing

- Test a limited number of products to identify winners.
- Scale your efforts as you gather sales data.
- Work with suppliers to create custom-branded products.
- Increases perceived value and builds brand loyalty.
- Relying on a single supplier is risky; have backups to avoid disruptions.
- Study competitors' best-selling items to identify potential opportunities.

6. Common Mistakes to Avoid

- **Choosing Oversaturated Products**: Avoid items everyone is selling unless you have a unique angle.
- **Ignoring Shipping Times**: Long shipping times can lead to customer dissatisfaction.

- **Skipping Product Testing**: Selling untested products can lead to quality issues and returns.

FBA Setup

Setting up Fulfillment by Amazon (FBA) allows sellers to leverage Amazon's extensive fulfillment network to store, pack, and ship products, as well as handle customer service and returns. Here's a step-by-step guide to get started:

1. Enroll in FBA

- **Access Seller Central**: Log in to your Seller Central account.
- **Set Up FBA**: Navigate to the 'Settings' menu, select 'Account Info,' and then 'Your Services.' Click 'Manage' and opt to 'Register for FBA.'

2. Prepare Your Products

- **Labeling**: Each product requires a unique scannable barcode (UPC, EAN, or ISBN). If your products don't have barcodes, you can use Amazon's FBA Label Service for a fee.
- **Packaging**: Ensure products are packaged according to Amazon's guidelines to prevent damage during storage and shipping.

3. Change Fulfillment Method

1. **Select the Product**: Next to the product, click the **Edit** button under the "Actions" column.
2. **Convert to FBA**: Choose the option **"Change to Fulfilled by Amazon"** from the dropdown menu.

4. Send Inventory to Amazon

- **Create a Shipment Plan**: In Seller Central, navigate to 'Inventory' > 'Manage FBA Shipments' > 'Send/Replenish Inventory.'
- **Prepare Shipment**: Specify the products, quantities, and shipping method.
- **Ship Products**: Print the provided shipping labels and send your products to the designated Amazon fulfillment center.

5. Monitor Your Inventory

- **Inventory Management**: Regularly check your inventory levels in Seller Central to ensure products remain in stock.
- **Replenishment**: Set up automatic alerts or restock reminders to maintain optimal inventory levels.

By following these steps, you can effectively set up and manage your FBA business, leveraging Amazon's logistics and customer service to enhance your selling experience.

Set Up FBA Fulfillment With Your Supplier

Setting up **Fulfillment by Amazon (FBA)** with your supplier involves coordinating product delivery to Amazon's fulfillment centers, ensuring compliance with Amazon's guidelines, and optimizing the process for seamless operations. Here's a step-by-step guide:

1. Understand FBA Basics

FBA allows Amazon to handle storage, packaging, shipping, and customer service for your products. Key benefits include:

- Prime eligibility for your products.
- Faster delivery options for customers.
- Amazon managing returns and customer inquiries.

2. Choose a Reliable Supplier

Work with a supplier who understands FBA requirements:

- **Experience with FBA:** Suppliers familiar with FBA processes can ensure compliance with labeling, packaging, and shipping guidelines.
- **Quality Assurance:** Ensure the supplier provides high-quality products consistently.
- **Reliable Lead Times:** Confirm production and delivery timelines to prevent stockouts at fulfillment centers.

3. Create Your Amazon Seller Account

If you haven't already:

1. Sign up for an Amazon Seller Central account.
2. Choose a **Professional** account for access to FBA features.
3. Configure your account for FBA by enabling FBA settings in Seller Central.

4. Prepare Your Products for FBA

Work with your supplier to meet Amazon's product preparation standards:

- **Packaging:** Ensure products are properly packaged to prevent damage during transit.
- **Labeling:**
    - Each item needs an **FNSKU (Fulfillment Network Stock Keeping Unit)** label provided by Amazon.
    - Discuss with your supplier if they can print and apply FNSKU labels, or you can have Amazon do it for a fee.
- **Compliance:** Ensure the products meet Amazon's safety, legal, and quality standards (e.g., no hazardous materials unless approved).

5. Create a Shipment Plan in Seller Central

Once your products are ready:

1. **Add Products to Inventory:**
   - Log in to Seller Central and navigate to **Inventory > Add a Product** or upload a bulk file if listing multiple products.
2. **Set Quantity and Prepare Shipment:**
   - Go to **Send to Amazon** under your inventory.
   - Enter product quantities and select your shipping method (small parcel delivery or pallet delivery).
3. **Generate Labels:**
   - Print shipping labels and send them to your supplier.

6. Coordinate with Your Supplier

Work with your supplier to:

- **Pack and Ship Directly to Amazon:** Provide them with the shipping plan and labels for direct delivery to Amazon's fulfillment centers.
- **Use Third-Party Prep Services:** If the supplier cannot prepare products for FBA, consider hiring a third-party service to handle labeling, packaging, and delivery.

7. Monitor Shipment to Fulfillment Centers

Track the shipment to ensure timely delivery:

- **Carrier Coordination:** Use Amazon-partnered carriers (e.g., UPS, FedEx) or freight services.

- **Track Progress:** Check shipment status in Seller Central to ensure products are received without delays.

Exporting from China to FBA

1. Shipping Methods from China to FBA

You have two main options for shipping products from China to Amazon FBA:

a. Air Freight

- **Faster but More Expensive**: Air freight is faster than sea freight, typically taking 7–15 days, but it's more expensive. It's suitable for smaller, urgent shipments.
- **Customs and Import Fees**: Ensure that all customs duties and taxes are paid before the goods arrive in the U.S. or other destination countries.
- **Choose a Freight Forwarder**: Use freight forwarders who specialize in Amazon FBA shipments. They can help you manage shipping logistics and provide necessary documentation.

b. Sea Freight (Container Shipping)

- **More Affordable for Larger Orders**: Sea freight is more cost-effective for larger shipments but can take between 20 to 60 days depending on the route.

- **Full Container Load (FCL) or Less than Container Load (LCL)**: For large orders, consider FCL, where you book an entire container, or LCL, where your goods share a container with others, lowering costs.
- **Shipping Costs and Customs Clearance**: The shipping cost will depend on the volume and weight of your shipment. Work with a freight forwarder to manage customs clearance.

2. Hire a Freight Forwarder and Customs Broker

- **Freight Forwarder**: A freight forwarder handles the logistics of shipping your products from China to the FBA warehouse. They help book transport, arrange the pickup from your supplier, and track your shipment.
- **Customs Broker**: A customs broker handles all customs paperwork and ensures that your goods are cleared for entry into the destination country, including paying any import duties and taxes.

Freight forwarders and customs brokers often offer packages that include both services, which can simplify the shipping process.

3. Prepare Documentation

- **Commercial Invoice**: This document lists the goods and their value. You will need this for customs clearance.
- **Packing List**: A detailed list of what's in each shipment, including quantity and weight.

- **Bill of Lading (BOL)**: A receipt from the shipping company that outlines the terms of the shipping agreement.
- **Import Declaration**: A document required for U.S. customs clearance, provided by your customs broker.
- **FBA Shipment Plan**: Created through your Amazon Seller Central account, this plan provides details on where your products will be shipped and their quantity.

4. Create an Amazon FBA Shipment Plan

- Log in to your Amazon Seller Central account.
- Go to **Inventory > Manage FBA Shipments**.
- Create a shipment plan, specifying the number of products, their dimensions, and the destination fulfillment centers (Amazon will assign this).
- Amazon will generate shipment labels and give you the FBA warehouse addresses.
- Once the shipment is ready, provide the shipment plan to your freight forwarder.

5. Ship Products to Amazon FBA

- Once you've arranged transportation and obtained all required documentation, your freight forwarder will ship the goods from China to Amazon's FBA fulfillment center.
- Use a **tracking number** to monitor your shipment's progress, and confirm with your forwarder that everything is on track.

- On arrival at the FBA center, Amazon will check the goods and inventory and make them available for sale.

6. Track and Manage Inventory

- Once your products arrive at Amazon FBA, monitor your inventory levels via your Seller Central account to ensure that your stock is available and ready for sale.
- Use **automated reordering** systems to ensure that your stock remains steady and avoid stockouts.

7. Pay Attention to Customs and Import Duties

- Be aware of customs duties and import taxes that apply when shipping goods from China to your destination country. The exact fees depend on your product type, value, and the country's regulations.
- Your customs broker will help you navigate this, but it's essential to budget for these costs as part of your overall product cost structure.

8. Review Your Shipping Process

- After your first shipment, evaluate the process and identify any challenges or areas for improvement. This could include finding faster shipping methods, lowering costs, or optimizing inventory management.

Tips for Success:

- **Choose Reliable Partners**: Work with a reputable freight forwarder, customs broker, and supplier to ensure smooth shipping and avoid complications.
- **Consider Seasonality**: Plan shipments in advance, especially during peak seasons like Amazon Prime Day, Black Friday, or the holiday shopping season.
- **Cost Efficiency**: Always look for cost-effective ways to ship (e.g., consolidating shipments, choosing the right shipping method).
- **Stay Informed**: Regularly check Amazon's FBA and shipping guidelines to ensure compliance with any changes.

By following these steps and working with the right partners, you can streamline the process of exporting products from China to Amazon FBA and build a successful, scalable business.

Manage FBA Customer Service

Managing **FBA (Fulfillment by Amazon)** customer service effectively is essential for maintaining high customer satisfaction and ensuring compliance with Amazon's standards. Amazon handles much of the customer service for FBA orders, but you still play a crucial role in certain areas. Here's a comprehensive guide:

1. Understand Amazon's Role in FBA Customer Service

Amazon manages most customer service aspects for FBA orders, including:

- **Order Processing:** Handling shipping, tracking, and delivery updates.
- **Returns and Refunds:** Managing return requests and issuing refunds as per their policies.
- **Customer Inquiries:** Addressing questions related to shipping, delivery status, and Prime benefits.

2. Focus on Areas You Control

While Amazon handles much of the process, sellers are responsible for:

Product Listings

- **Accurate Descriptions:** Ensure your listings provide complete and accurate product details.
- **Images and Information:** Use high-quality images and clear descriptions to minimize customer confusion or dissatisfaction.
- **Answering Product Questions:** Respond to customer questions in the Q&A section of your product listings to provide clarity and build trust.

Product Quality

- **Inspect Products:** Ensure your supplier delivers high-quality, defect-free products to Amazon fulfillment centers.
- **Handle Complaints:** Work with your supplier to address quality issues if customers report defective or unsatisfactory items.

3. Monitor Customer Feedback

Regularly review and respond to customer feedback:

- **Product Reviews:**
    - Address negative reviews tactfully by offering solutions or clarifying misunderstandings.
    - Use feedback to identify areas for improvement.
- **Seller Feedback:**
    - Respond to feedback about your service or product to show customers you care.

4. Handle Customer Returns and Refunds

Although Amazon processes returns for FBA orders, you should:

- **Understand Return Reasons:**
    - Review return reports in Seller Central to identify recurring issues.
    - Collaborate with your supplier to address product defects or inconsistencies.

- **Provide Support for Issues Outside Amazon's Policy:**
  - For specific cases, such as warranty claims or technical support, assist customers directly.

5. Maintain Communication

Amazon requires you to communicate effectively in areas they don't handle:

- **Customer Messages:** Respond to customer inquiries related to your brand, product specifics, or additional information not covered by Amazon.
- **Timely Responses:** Reply to messages within **24 hours** to avoid negative impacts on your seller performance metrics.

6. Monitor Account Health Metrics

Keep an eye on key performance metrics that reflect your customer service quality:

- **Order Defect Rate (ODR):** Keep negative feedback, chargebacks, and A-to-Z claims below 1%.
- **Customer Feedback Rating:** Strive for positive reviews and ratings.
- **Return Dissatisfaction Rate:** Ensure returns are processed smoothly to avoid customer complaints.

7. Proactively Prevent Issues

Anticipate and address potential customer service challenges:

- **Stock Availability:** Maintain inventory levels to prevent stockouts and delays.
- **Delivery Speed:** Ensure FBA inventory is replenished regularly to keep delivery times fast, especially for Prime customers.
- **Packaging Quality:** Use durable and appropriate packaging to minimize damage during shipping.

8. Resolve A-to-Z Guarantee Claims

If a customer files an **A-to-Z Guarantee claim**, you may need to get involved:

- **Review Claims Promptly:** Provide Amazon with any requested information or documentation.
- **Resolve Issues Quickly:** Work to resolve the issue directly with the customer, if possible.

9. Use FBA Reports for Insights

Leverage reports in Seller Central to improve customer service:

- **Returns Reports:** Understand why customers return products and take corrective action.
- **Customer Feedback Reports:** Track feedback trends to identify and address common issues.
- **Performance Notifications:** Stay informed about customer complaints or policy violations.

10. Escalate to Amazon Support When Necessary

For issues you cannot resolve, escalate the matter to Amazon Seller Support:

- **Contact Support:** Provide clear details about the customer's concern and any actions you've already taken.
- **Follow Up:** Ensure the issue is resolved to the customer's satisfaction.

11. Build Your Brand with Proactive Engagement

- **Provide Additional Resources:** Offer user guides, FAQs, or instructional videos through your Amazon storefront or Enhanced Brand Content (EBC/A+ Content).
- **Encourage Reviews:** Politely request feedback from customers, adhering to Amazon's review policy.

By staying proactive, monitoring performance, and addressing issues quickly, you can ensure that FBA customer service meets both Amazon's standards and your customers' expectations.

FBA Product Removal

FBA Product Removal refers to the process of removing inventory from Amazon's fulfillment centers. If you're an

Amazon FBA seller, there may be situations where you need to remove products, such as:

1. **Aging Inventory**: Products that haven't sold within a specific timeframe to avoid long-term storage fees.
2. **Defective or Damaged Items**: Items that can no longer be sold or need to be returned.
3. **Excess Inventory**: Overstocked items to make space for more profitable products.
4. **Unsellable Inventory**: Items marked as unsellable due to customer returns or damage.
5. **Discontinued Products**: Items you no longer wish to sell.

Steps to Remove FBA Inventory

1. **Log in to Seller Central**: Navigate to the **Manage Inventory** page under the **Inventory** tab.
2. **Select Products**: Identify the products you want to remove.
3. **Create a Removal Order**:
   - Click on the dropdown next to the product and select **Create Removal Order**.
   - Choose the **Return** option (ship back to your address) or **Dispose** (Amazon will discard the products for you).
4. **Provide Shipping Details**: If you're returning the inventory, input your address for shipment.
5. **Confirm Removal**: Submit the removal order. Amazon will process it, and you'll receive tracking information if items are returned.

Fees for Removal

Amazon charges fees for removing inventory:

- **Return Fees**: Cost to send products back to your address.
- **Disposal Fees**: Cost for Amazon to dispose of unsellable inventory.

Tips for FBA Product Removal

- **Monitor Inventory Age**: Regularly check your inventory to avoid long-term storage fees.
- **Bundle or Discount Slow-Moving Items**: Before opting for removal, consider bundling slow sellers or offering discounts to clear them.
- **Plan Ahead**: Removal orders can take up to 10–14 days to process.

Amazon Drop Shipping Challenges And Risks

While dropshipping on Amazon offers an easy entry point into e-commerce, it also comes with specific challenges and risks that require careful management. Below are the key challenges and risks you should be aware of:

1. Account Suspension and Policy Violations

Amazon has strict policies that govern dropshipping, and failure to comply can result in account suspension. Common violations include:

- **Selling without being the seller of record**: Amazon requires you to be the seller of record, meaning you must be listed as the seller on all packing slips and invoices. If your supplier's information appears, it can violate Amazon's dropshipping policy.
- **Failure to fulfill orders within Amazon's guidelines**: If you don't ship products promptly or provide adequate customer service, your account can be suspended.
- **Not managing returns properly**: If you don't have a clear process in place for returns, Amazon may penalize you for poor service.

Tip: Always review and follow Amazon's **dropshipping policy** carefully to avoid any violations.

2. Reliance on Third-Party Suppliers

Your dropshipping business depends entirely on your supplier to deliver products on time and meet quality standards. Problems with your supplier can directly affect your business:

- **Stock Issues**: If your supplier runs out of stock and you don't have control over inventory levels, you risk canceling orders or disappointing customers.

- **Quality Control**: If the supplier sends poor-quality products or makes mistakes, it's your reputation that suffers.
- **Shipping Delays**: Relying on third-party supplier's means delays in shipping and missed deadlines, which can lead to negative customer feedback.
- **Lack of Communication**: If the supplier doesn't communicate effectively regarding stock levels, delays, or product issues, it can cause operational problems.

Tip: Vet suppliers carefully and maintain good communication. Consider having backup suppliers.

3. Low Profit Margins

Dropshipping often involves lower profit margins compared to holding inventory. Because you're sourcing products from a supplier and selling them at a retail price, the markup is often small. Additionally:

- **Amazon Fees**: Amazon charges fees for storage, fulfillment (FBA), and other services, which can eat into your margins.
- **Competition**: Many sellers may be offering the same or similar products, which can drive prices down.
- **Advertising Costs**: If you're using Amazon Ads, the cost per click (CPC) can impact profitability if not managed well.

Tip: Focus on products with higher margins, differentiate your offering with unique features, and optimize your Amazon ads to maximize ROI.

4. Customer Service Challenges

While Amazon handles many aspects of customer service for FBA orders, dropshipping requires you to manage issues directly, including:

- **Managing Returns:** If a customer returns a product, you need to handle the return process and ensure the supplier accepts it and processes the refund.
- **Negative Reviews:** Customer complaints about product quality, delayed shipments, or incorrect orders can lead to poor reviews, damaging your store's reputation.
- **Customer Expectations:** As a dropshipper, you don't control shipping speeds or product quality, which can make it harder to meet customer expectations.

Tip: Establish clear communication with your suppliers to handle customer issues promptly and professionally.

5. Complicated Tax and Legal Issues

Dropshipping across borders or selling in multiple regions may create tax challenges:

- **Sales Tax:** You must understand how sales tax applies in different states or countries, as Amazon may collect sales tax on your behalf in some regions but not all.

- **International Regulations**: Selling to international customers may require navigating customs duties, import/export laws, and other legalities.
- **VAT and Other Taxes**: Depending on where you're selling, you may need to manage VAT (Value Added Tax) or other local taxes.

Tip: Consult with a tax advisor or legal professional to ensure you're compliant with tax regulations in all the regions where you operate.

6. Inventory Synchronization Issues

Since you're not physically handling the inventory, it can be challenging to keep track of stock levels:

- **Out-of-Stock Items**: If the supplier runs out of stock, and you don't monitor inventory levels regularly, you may continue selling products that are unavailable, resulting in canceled orders or dissatisfied customers.
- **Overstocking**: If you're working with multiple suppliers, managing inventory levels across different suppliers can be complex.

Tip: Use inventory management software or dropshipping platforms that sync product availability with your suppliers and alert you when items are out of stock.

7. Shipping Complexities

Shipping products from various suppliers can lead to complications:

- **Multiple Shipments**: If you sell products from multiple suppliers, customers may receive multiple packages, which can confuse or frustrate them.
- **Long Shipping Times**: Some dropshipping suppliers may offer long shipping times, which can affect customer satisfaction, especially for Prime customers who expect fast delivery.

Tip: Clearly communicate expected shipping times to customers and offer tracking information. Consider suppliers with faster shipping methods or use Amazon's FBA to ensure faster deliveries.

8. Branding and Differentiation

Since you're selling products from third-party suppliers, it can be difficult to establish a unique brand:

- **Lack of Control Over Product Quality**: Your ability to improve or change product designs or features is limited.
- **Generic Listings**: Many dropshipping products are the same across different stores, which can make it hard to stand out in a crowded market.

Tip: Consider branding your own products, using custom packaging, or offering bundle deals that make your products stand out from the competition.

9. Scaling Issues

While dropshipping is easy to start, scaling the business effectively can be difficult:

- **Supplier Limitations**: As your sales increase, some suppliers may struggle to meet demand, leading to delays or errors.
- **Order Management**: As you scale, manually managing orders, tracking inventory, and dealing with customer service can become overwhelming without automation tools.
- **Shipping Costs**: As you grow, the cost of shipping, especially for international orders, can eat into profits.

Tip: Automate processes where possible, such as order management and customer service, and work with reliable suppliers who can scale with you.

10. Market Saturation

Amazon is highly competitive, and many dropshipping niches are saturated:

- **Price Wars**: Competing against many sellers who offer the same products can lead to price wars, making it harder to maintain healthy margins.
- **Advertising Costs**: Higher competition may increase the cost of running ads on Amazon, making it harder to remain profitable.

Tip: Niche down and look for specific target audiences, unique products, or underserved markets to reduce competition and stand out.

While Amazon dropshipping offers several advantages like low startup costs and no need for inventory management, it comes with significant challenges and risks. By choosing reliable suppliers, staying compliant with Amazon's policies, monitoring customer service, and carefully managing your business operations, you can mitigate these risks and increase the chances of success.

Scaling Your Business On Amazon

Scaling your business on Amazon requires a strategic approach, focusing on key areas to increase visibility, optimize operations, and improve profitability. Here are some steps and strategies to scale your Amazon business effectively:

1. Optimize Product Listings

- **Title & Keywords**: Use high-performing keywords that potential customers are searching for. Optimize your product titles, descriptions, and bullet points for both relevance and conversion.
- **Images**: High-quality images are essential for attracting customers. Ensure your product images

meet Amazon's standards and showcase the product from multiple angles.
- **A+ Content (Enhanced Brand Content)**: Utilize A+ Content to enhance your product description with rich media, better formatting, and compelling storytelling, which can improve conversion rates.

2. Expand Product Range

- **Diversify**: Introduce new products related to your existing range. Use customer feedback, market trends, and competitor analysis to identify opportunities.
- **Private Label or Exclusive Products**: Consider private labeling or developing exclusive products. This allows you to build a brand that stands out and reduces reliance on other sellers.
- **Bundle Products**: Create product bundles that offer customers more value while increasing your average order value.

3. Optimize Pricing

- **Competitive Pricing**: Regularly monitor your competitors' prices and adjust accordingly to stay competitive while ensuring profitability.
- **Dynamic Pricing**: Use automated pricing tools to adjust your prices based on competition, demand, and other factors, keeping your pricing strategy optimized at all times.

4. Utilize Amazon FBA (Fulfilled by Amazon)

- **Outsource Fulfillment**: Let Amazon handle storage, packing, and shipping, so you can focus on scaling your business. FBA also gives you access to Prime customers.
- **Maximize Inventory Management**: Efficiently manage your inventory to avoid stockouts and overstocking, both of which can hurt your sales and account health.
- **Increase Sales with FBA Advantages**: Amazon's FBA program offers faster shipping, higher visibility, and customer trust, all of which can lead to better sales.

5. Leverage Amazon Advertising

- **Amazon PPC (Pay-Per-Click)**: Run targeted PPC campaigns such as Sponsored Products, Sponsored Brands, and Sponsored Display to increase visibility and drive sales.
- **Optimized Ad Campaigns**: Continuously monitor and optimize your ad campaigns. Test different keywords, targeting strategies, and bidding strategies to improve your ROI.
- **External Traffic**: Drive external traffic to your Amazon listings through social media, email marketing, or influencers. This can improve sales and organic ranking on Amazon.

6. Enhance Customer Experience

- **Customer Service**: Provide excellent customer service by responding quickly to questions and addressing

complaints. This helps maintain a positive seller rating and customer loyalty.
- **Manage Reviews**: Encourage happy customers to leave reviews, and actively monitor and respond to feedback. This helps build trust and improves your product's ranking.
- **Handle Returns and Claims Efficiently**: Efficiently manage returns and A-to-Z claims to avoid negative impacts on your seller performance.

7. Focus on Branding

- **Create a Brand Store**: Set up an Amazon Brand Store to create a cohesive shopping experience that showcases your brand and products.
- **Amazon Brand Registry**: Enroll in Amazon Brand Registry to protect your brand from counterfeiters and gain access to enhanced marketing tools.
- **Social Media & Influencer Partnerships**: Build your brand's presence off Amazon through social media platforms and influencer collaborations to drive more traffic to your listings.

8. Expand to International Markets

- **Sell Globally**: Take advantage of Amazon's global marketplaces to expand into new markets. Use Amazon's Global Selling Program to list your products in multiple countries and reach a broader customer base.

- **Localized Listings**: Tailor your listings to fit local languages, currencies, and preferences to better connect with international customers.

9. Improve Operational Efficiency

- **Automate Processes**: Use tools for inventory management, order processing, and customer service to save time and reduce human error.
- **Outsource Tasks**: As you scale, consider outsourcing tasks like customer service, product photography, or even hiring virtual assistants to handle routine tasks.
- **Streamline Logistics**: Work on optimizing shipping processes and manage supply chain efficiently to avoid delays and disruptions.

10. Monitor Key Performance Indicators (KPIs)

- **Track Metrics**: Regularly monitor key metrics such as conversion rate, advertising spend, inventory levels, order defect rate, and overall account health.
- **Review Performance Analytics**: Use Amazon's Seller Central tools and third-party analytics platforms to get insights into your sales trends and identify areas for improvement.

11. Leverage Amazon's Promotional Tools

- **Discounts & Coupons**: Run time-limited promotions or offer coupons to increase sales during peak shopping seasons or to drive traffic to new products.

- **Lightning Deals & Prime Day**: Participate in Lightning Deals, Black Friday, Cyber Monday, and Prime Day to boost sales and brand visibility.

12. Stay Compliant and Up-to-Date

- **Amazon Policies**: Keep yourself updated with Amazon's policies, rules, and regulations to avoid penalties or account suspension.
- **Tax Compliance**: Ensure you comply with tax regulations in different regions to avoid issues with sales tax.

Scaling your Amazon business requires a combination of strategic planning, consistent execution, and leveraging Amazon's vast tools and resources. By continuously improving your operations and marketing strategies, you can grow your sales and expand your business successfully.

Monitoring Amazon Performance Metrics

Monitoring Amazon FBA performance metrics is essential for optimizing your sales and maintaining a healthy account. Amazon provides several key metrics that help you track the performance of your FBA operations. Here are some of the key metrics to monitor:

1. Order Defect Rate (ODR)

- This metric tracks the percentage of orders that have defects, including negative feedback, A-to-Z claims, and chargeback claims. Amazon expects this to be below 1%.

2. Pre-Fulfillment Cancel Rate

- This is the percentage of orders that are canceled by the seller before shipment. Amazon recommends keeping this rate under 2.5%.

3. Late Shipment Rate (LSR)

- This tracks the percentage of orders shipped late. To maintain a good seller standing, Amazon recommends keeping this rate below 4%.

4. Perfect Order Percentage

- This measures the percentage of orders that are delivered without any issues, including on-time delivery, no defects, and no customer complaints. Higher values here are better.

5. Customer Satisfaction

- Amazon tracks customer feedback and reviews. You should aim to maintain a high average rating for your products, generally 4.5 stars or higher.

6. Inventory Performance Index (IPI)

- The IPI score measures the health of your inventory and efficiency. It takes into account factors like stranded inventory, excess inventory, and sell-through rate. A higher IPI indicates better inventory management.

7. Return Rate

- This metric tracks the percentage of products returned by customers. A high return rate can indicate product issues or poor fit with customer expectations, which can negatively affect your seller rating.

8. Fulfillment Fees

- Monitoring your FBA fulfillment fees helps you understand the cost of using Amazon's FBA service. The fees include storage costs and fulfillment charges based on product size and weight.

9. Shipments and Tracking Accuracy

- Ensuring that your shipments are properly tracked and processed is crucial for customer satisfaction. Monitor the accuracy and timeliness of your shipments.

10. FBA Inventory Health

- This shows how well your products are selling, how much inventory is available, and how much inventory is aging. Optimizing inventory turnover is key to reducing costs associated with long-term storage fees.

11. Amazon Seller Performance Dashboard

- This provides a consolidated view of your account health, including all the metrics mentioned above. You should check this regularly to stay informed about your overall performance.

By regularly monitoring these metrics, you can maintain good seller health, optimize your operations, and ensure that you're providing a positive experience for your customers.

Amazon Glossary

- **1P** – First Party, describes Amazon's direct relationship with manufacturer brands and distributors that receive purchase orders from the retailer (refers to Vendor Central).
- **3P** – Third-Party, describes sellers trading goods on Amazon's marketplace without selling these items to Amazon first (refers to Seller Central).
- **3PL** – Third-Party Logistics
- **3PS** – Third-Party Seller
- **A+ Content** – Product page with enhanced content features on Amazon, e.g., feature comparison tables, enhanced imagery, etc.
- **A2Z** – A-to-Z, guarantee customer protection
- **A9** – Shortened version of the word Algorithms ("A" followed by nine characters). Describes the search technology behind the Amazon product search.
- **AA** – Amazon Advertising
- **Acapulco** – Refers to Amazon Pallet Ordering.
- **ACoS** – Advertising Cost of Sale. Describes the ratio of your ad budget to your ad revenue. ACoS = total ad spend ÷ total ad revenue.
- **ACU** – Average Cost per Unit. The average weighted cost price for which Amazon has ordered a product in a given time period.
- **AGS** – Amazon Global Store
- **AITBB** – Anything In The Buy Box
- **AMC** – Amazon Marketing Cloud

- **AMS** – Amazon Marketing Services, now known as Sponsored Ads.
- **AMG** – Amazon Media Group, now known as Amazon Ads.
- **AMZ, AMZN or AZ** – Amazon
- **AMZL** – Amazon Logistics
- **AMZNCC** – Amazon Carton Content Code. External Container ID to label cartons to be sent to Amazon and generated via Vendor Central.
- **Andon Cord** – If customers report a product as dangerous or as repeatedly delivered damaged, customer service representatives will remove a product's listing from the website until the cause is identified and resolved.
- **AP** – Accounts Payable
- **API** – Application Programming Interface. Allows computers to communicate with each other, often used between Amazon and its suppliers.
- **ARA** – Amazon Retail Analytics, also referred to as ARA basic. A data reporting section in Vendor Central that brands can access to analyse their sales and inventory with Amazon.
- **ARAP** – Amazon Retail Analytics Premium. A now-deprecated reporting section that allowed vendors to analyse customer behaviour and traffic on product pages.
- **ARN** – Amazon Reference Number. Used for Collect (WePay) shipments only.
- **ASIN** – Amazon Standard Identification Number. A unique 10-character alphanumeric identifier for

a product on Amazon (for example, B07ZB5C3ZM). It is linked to a unique SKU/EAN/ISBN code and is used as a reference to manage catalogue attributes, prices and inventory of a product.
- **ASN** – Advanced Shipment Notification. A document that notifies Amazon about the time and characteristics of a pending shipment.
- **ASP** – Average Selling Price. Calculated by net sales ÷ volume sold.
- **ATC** – Add to Cart
- **AVN** – Annual Vendor Negotiation. Describes the yearly alignment of terms between Amazon and its 1P suppliers.
- **AVS** – Amazon Vendor Service, formerly known as Strategic Vendor Service (SVS). It's a paid programme that gives vendors access to a dedicated contact to assist with operational matters such as ordering and catalogue.
- **AW** – Amazon Warehouse
- **AWS** – Amazon Web Services
- **B2B** – Business to Business
- **B2C** – Business to Consumer
- **BA** – Brand Analytics. Dashboard for brand owners registered with Amazon's Brand Registry to understand the wider performance of their brand (not account) on the Amazon marketplace.
- **BB** – Buy Box. Refers to the Amazon product detail page area where customers can choose to add products to their shopping cart.

- **BD** – Best Deal. A type of price discount on Amazon that runs several days or weeks.
- **BISS** – Business Industrial & Scientific Supplies. A category on Amazon that targets sales to industrial and scientific customers.
- **BOGO** – Buy One Get One. A promotion type for sellers.
- **BOL** – Bill of Landing. Document issued by a carrier that serves three purposes: 1) serves as a receipt for the goods delivered to the carrier for shipment, 2) defines the contract of carriage of the goods from the point of origin to the point of destination according to the responsibilities of the service provider listed on the bill of lading, 3) under certain conditions, provides evidence of title for the goods.
- **Brand Analytics** – Dashboard for brand owners registered with Amazon's Brand Registry to understand the wider performance of their brand (not account) on the Amazon marketplace.
- **Brand Registry** – Programme for brands to verify their brand to access enhanced analytics and brand protection features.
- **Brand Store** – Part of Amazon Advertising. Brands can create a free store, showcasing their products with customisable images, logos and content.
- **Browse Node** – A numerical code to identify an Amazon product category.

- **BTR** – Born to Run. A programme that allows vendors to request an initial purchase order for new products from Amazon.
- **BTS** – Back to School
- **BSR** – Best Seller Rank
- **Bundle** – Multiple single items that can be identified with different EAN/ASIN codes sold together as a single offering.
- **Buy Box** – Refers to the area on the Amazon product detail page where customers can choose to add products to their shopping cart.
- **BWP** – Buy with Prime. A service that allows brands to sell through their online shop using Amazon's order processing for end customers.
- **CAGR** – Compound Annual Growth Rate
- **CARP** – Carrier Appointment Request Portal
- **Category Page** – A landing page for product groups within the Amazon store. Examples include Home & Furniture, Grocery, Beauty, etc.
- **Chargeback** – Describes a penalty that Amazon charges for non-compliance with standardised processes or late/inaccurate product deliveries.
- **Child ASIN** – Describes a product listed under a parent ASIN (e.g., chocolate bar). The child ASINs are the variations under this parent ASIN (e.g., dark/white/milk flavour).
- **Chime** – Amazon's instant messenger that lets employees and brands meet, chat, and place business calls inside and outside their organisation.

- **Climate Pledge Friendly** – Amazon's programme to visibly mark eco-friendly and sustainable products on its marketplace.
- **CM** – Contribution Margin. The formula: (Average Selling Price – Average Cost per Unit + Contra-COGS – Var. Costs) ÷ Average Selling Price.
- **Co-op or Coop** – Short for cooperative marketing. Also referred to as Automated Marketing on Amazon.
- **COGS** – Costs of Goods Sold. The value of goods sold during a selected time period.
- **Contra COGS** – The money vendors spend with Amazon to offset COGS. Calculated based on the cost price (list price) at which a product is sold to Amazon.
- **Concessions** – The dollar amount Amazon has refunded to customers.
- **Coupon (also: Vendor Powered Coupon, or VPC)** – A type of discount vendors and sellers can offer to customers. Customers redeem the coupons on the product detail page.
- **CP** – Contribution Profit. The dollar value of the Contribution Margin.
- **CPC** – Cost per Click. Measures the dollar amount Amazon Advertising charges vendors and sellers when customers click on their ads.
- **CPQ** – Case Pack Quantity.
- **CR** – Confirmation Rate

- **CRAP** – Cannot Realise Any Profit. Products that got delisted because they are unprofitable to Amazon.
- **CSA** – Cost Support Agreement
- **CTC** – Contribution to Change
- **CTR** – Click-through Rate. Calculated as the number of clicks ÷ number of impressions.
- **CS** – Customer Service
- **CX** – Customer Experience
- **DA** – Damage Allowance
- **Deal OPS** – Revenue generated by deals and promotions run with Amazon.
- **DF** – Direct Fulfilment
- **DI** – Direct Import
- **DOTD** – Deal of the Day. A type of promotion for vendors to discount a product for up to 24 hours during key deal events (e.g., Prime Day, Black Friday, Cyber Monday, etc.). Nowadays also known as "Top Deal".
- **DP** – Detail Page. The product page for an ASIN on Amazon.
- **DSP** – Demand Side Platform. A platform that enables brands to programmatically buy display and video ads.
- **DPV** – Detail Page Views. The number of impressions of a detail page in a selected time period.
- **DSP** – Demand Side Platform. Amazon's display advertising programme.

- **EAN** – The International Article Number is a standard describing a barcode symbology and numbering system used in global trade to identify a specific retail product type, in a specific packaging configuration, from a specific manufacturer.
- **EBC** – Enhanced Brand Content. The seller equivalent of A+ Content that is available to Amazon vendors.
- **ECDD** – Estimated Cargo Delivery Date
- **EDD** – Estimated Delivery Date
- **EDI** – Electronic Data Interchange. A method to send digital information between companies, mainly used to receive and process purchasing orders.
- **EOD** – End of Day
- **EFN** – European Fulfilment Network. Enables brands to sell across European marketplaces while only delivering to Amazon in their home country.
- **FBA** – Fulfilment by Amazon. Programme for 3P sellers who let Amazon handle and ship their products to end customers.
- **FBM** – Fulfiled by Merchant. Refers to 3P sellers shipping products directly to the end customer.
- **FC** – Fulfilment Center. Describes Amazon's warehouses.
- **FFP** – Frustration-Free Packaging. An Amazon programme aimed at eliminating excessive and difficult-to-open packaging.

- **FLOW** – Forward-Looking Order Workflow. Amazon purchase orders with a shipping window for a future week for best-selling products.
- **FNSKU** – Fulfillment Network Stock Keeping Unit. Identifies products fulfilled by Amazon.
- **FOB** – Free on Board. Relates to the Direct Import model with Amazon, under which vendors are responsible for all costs until the goods are on the vessel at the designated port.
- **Gated Product** – Refers to products that are blocked for sale by 3P sellers on the Amazon marketplace.
- **GDSN** – Global Data Synchronization Network. A tool that allows catalogue updates with Amazon.
- **GL** – General Ledger. Describes the P&L of the main product category (e.g. Home, Consumer Electronics, Beauty, etc.)
- **Glance Views** – Equivalent to the number of impressions of a product detail page.
- **GMS** – Gross Merchandise Sales
- **GMV** – Gross Merchandising Value
- **Goldbox** – Refers to Amazon's deals & promotions page.
- **GPE** – Global Procurement Excellence
- **GTIN** – Global Trade Item Number (GTIN). A 14-digit code that uniquely identifies products, items and services.
- **H1** – First half of the year
- **H2** – Second half of the year
- **HB** – Heavy Bulky

- **HTD** – Half Year to Date
- **Hazmat** – Hazardous materials. Refers to highly flammable, toxic or pressurised items that must therefore be handled with special care to protect the health of employees and customers.
- **IDQ** – Item Data Quality. Used to spot product listings with missing titles, bullet points or other content features that need improvement.
- **Incoterms** – International Commercial Terms
- **Impressions** – Describes the number of views of a product page.
- **IOR** – Importer of Record
- **IPCP** – Inbound Preferred Carrier Programme
- **IP** – Intellectual Property
- **IPIP** – Items Per Inner Pack
- **IPMP** – Inner Packs Per Master Pack
- **ISA** – Inbound Shipment Appointment
- **ISBN** – International Standard Book Number. A 13-digit number assigned to identify products in a catalogue. Similar to EAN/SKU.
- **IXD** – Inbound Crossdock. An Amazon warehouse that accepts freight from vendors/sellers and ships product to various fulfillment centers. IXDs do not ship customer orders.
- **JBP** – Joint Business Plan. Describes the commercial alignment between Amazon and 1P vendors to review their performance and create a plan for growing their business together over a set period of time.

- **KPI** – Key Performance Indicator. A measurable value that shows how effective you are at achieving business objectives.
- **KVI** – Key Value Item
- **LBB** – Lost Buy Box
- **LD** – Lightning Deal. A type of discount on Amazon that is limited to 4-6 hours of running time.
- **LFO** –Lost Featured Offer. Expected to replace the Lost Buy Box metric in Amazon analytics dashboards in the future.
- **Listing Optimization** – Refers to the process of improving the content of a listing to improve its organic ranking in the Amazon search results.
- **LPR** – Licence Plate Receive. Receive process where items are received by scanning a barcode (SSCC / AMZNCC) on the outside of the package, thus eliminating the need to scan each item.
- **LSPL** – Large Scale Product Launch. A vendor-specific programme where Amazon increases inventory coverage for new items with no return policy but in exchange for advertising investments.
- **LTL** – Less than Truck Load
- **Marketplace** – The locale or domain in which Amazon is active. Examples are Amazon.co.uk, Amazon.de, etc.

- **MAP** – Minimum Advertised Price. Used by brands to ensure a product is not sold under a minimum set price (only applicable in the US).
- **MCF** – Multi-Channel Fulfillment. A service that allows brands to use Amazon warehouses to store and ship products sold outside of Amazon.
- **MCP** – Matching Compensation. Refers to Amazon's request to support low-margin products with investments to keep them listed in the catalogue.
- **MDF** – Marketing Discretionary Funding, or Market Development Funding. A trade term offered by Vendor Managers during annual negotiations.
- **MF** – Merchant Fulfilled. Refers to sellers shipping products directly to the end customer.
- **MOA** – Manufacturer on Amazon Policy.
- **MoM** – Month over Month
- **MOQ** – Minimum Order Quantity. Describes the minimum amount Amazon needs to order.
- **MP** – Marketplace
- **MPPP** – Master Packs Per Pallet
- **MTD** – Month to Date
- **MSRP** – Manufacturer's Suggested Retail Price
- **MWS** – Marketplace Web Services
- **NARF** – North American Remote Fulfilment
- **NAFN** – North American Fulfillment Network
- **NASP** – North American Selection Policy
- **NDA** – Non-Disclosure Agreement

- **Net PPM** – The ratio between your average selling price and cost price, which also considers any accruals and C-COGS a vendor has with Amazon. Calculated as (Average Selling Price – Average Cost per Unit + Contra-COGS) ÷ Average Selling Price (Net PPM calculator).
- **Net Receipts** – Expresses the volume received by Amazon multiplied by the vendor's cost price.
- **NIS** – New Item Setup. Describes the listing process of a product.
- **NP** – New product. Refers to a newly listed item.
- **NR** – Non-Replenish able. An item that cannot be restocked.
- **NTB** – Reflects whether an ad-attributed purchase was made by an existing or new customer.
- **OB** – Obsolete
- **OIH** – Order Inventory Health
- **Ordered Revenue** – Refers to the orders placed by end customers that have not yet shipped by Amazon. It's based on the average selling price at the time of the order. Calculated as: ASP * Volume Ordered.
- **Ordered Volume** – Equals Ordered Revenue ÷ ASP.
- **OMOQ** – Offer Minimum Order Quantity
- **OOS** – Out of Stock
- **OPS** – Ordered Product Sales, equivalent to Ordered Revenue
- **OTC** – Over the Counter

- **O2C** – Order to Cash. Describes the process that entails all aspects of handling the sale to Amazon. This includes shipping goods to Amazon, creating invoices, receiving payments, and reporting on the end-to-end process.
- **OTP** – One-Time Password
- **P70** – Amazon estimates with a 70% probability that future weekly customer demand will be at or below this value.
- **P80** – Amazon estimates with an 80% probability that future weekly customer demand will be at or below this value.
- **P90** – Amazon estimates with a 90% probability that future weekly customer demand will be at or below this value.
- **P&L** – Profit and Loss
- **Parent ASIN** – Describes the ASIN under which the variants of a product are grouped together. The parent ASIN could be a chocolate bar, while the child ASINs are the flavour variations (e.g., dark/white/milk flavour).
- **PBS** – Predictive Buying System
- **PCOGS** – Product Costs of Goods Sold. Expresses the quantity sold multiplied by the cost price of a vendor. PCOGs equal Shipped COGS in Vendor Central.
- **PDP** – Product Detail Page. The webpage a shopper views when browsing an item on Amazon.

- **PFR** – Provisions for Receivables. Describes an accounting tactic where Amazon prioritises its own cash flow and only pays vendor invoices when the sum of outstanding amounts from trade terms, chargebacks and financial disputes is less than the actual invoice amount from the vendor.
- **PIB** – Perfect Inbound. Describes the number of shipments that Amazon fulfilment centres can process quickly, without delays or problems.
- **PIBDR** – Perfect Inbound Defect Rate. Measures the number of inbound defects as a % of all received units at Amazon fulfilment centres.
- **PICS** – Pan European Inbound Consolidation Service. A logistics programme that helps vendors reduce the number of fulfilment centers they need to supply.
- **PLT** – Procurement Lead Time
- **PO** – Purchase Order
- **POC** – Point of Contact
- **POD** – Proof of Delivery
- **PPA** – Price Protection Agreement. Protects Amazon against a reduction in value of the units currently on hand and in transit.
- **PPC** –Pay Per Click. A type of Amazon Advertising where a brand pays when an ad gets clicked.
- **PPM** – Pure Profit Margin. Describes the ratio between the average selling price and cost price. In other words, it is the amount of money Amazon makes from the sale of a product before costs.

Calculated as (Average Selling Price − Average Cost per Unit) ÷ Average Selling Price.
- **PPOOS** − Procurable Product OOS. Describes the out of stock (OOS) rate on all products that are procurable. Procurable Product OOS = OOS Glance Views (GVs) on Procurable ASINS / Total GVs.
- **PPV** − Product Price Variation. When the cost price of a vendor invoice does not match the cost price of the Amazon purchase order.
- **PQV** − Product Quantity Variation. When the product quantity of a vendor invoice does not match the number of received items at the Amazon warehouse.
- **PR** − Planned Replenishment
- **Prime** − Amazon's subscription service for free delivery, which also entails services like Amazon Music and Video.
- **PRO** − Progressive Number. A tracking number that is issued by a carrier for its freight.
- **PL** − Private Label. Describes products sold by Amazon under their own brand name but made by other manufacturers.
- **Q1** − First Quarter (Jan-Mar)
- **Q2** − Second Quarter (Apr-Jun)
- **Q3** − Third Quarter (Jul-Sep)
- **Q4** − Fourth Quarter (Oct-Dec)
- **Q5** − Fifth Quarter. Refers to a hectic first quarter right after the Christmas period (colloq.).
- **QA** − Quality Assurance

- **QBR** – Quarterly Business Review
- **QD** – Quantity Discount. Applicable for sales with Amazon Business.
- **QUID** – Quantitative Ingredient Declaration
- **ROO** – Removal of Offer. Refers to the removal of the Buy Box, while active Subscribe and Save customers will continue to receive orders.
- **ROAS** – Return on Ad Spend. Describes how much revenue a brand gets in return for its advertising budget. Calculated as ROAS = 100 * total ad revenue ÷ total ad spend.
- **ROI** – Return on Investment
- **RRA** – Rapid Retail Analytics
- **RRP** – Recommended Retail Price
- **SAS** – Strategic Account Services. A programme that gives sellers access to a designated Amazon account manager to help them increase sales and optimise their business.
- **SBSAS** – Standards for Brands Selling in the Amazon Store Policy
- **SC** – Seller Central. The admin interface used to market and sell products directly to Amazon customers.
- **SCAC** – Standard Carrier Alpha Code
- **SCP** – Supply Chain Programme
- **SD** – Sales Discount. Describes amounts related to promotional activities that Amazon conducts at the customer checkout.
- **SDA** – Selective Distribution Agreement. Used by suppliers to maintain control over the resale of its

products by only selling to distributors meeting specific criteria.
- **SDN** – Selective Distribution Network. Describes the distributors that are part of an SDA.
- **SEO** – Search Engine Optimisation
- **SFP** – Seller Fulfiled Prime. Refers to sellers that ship products from their own warehouses and comply with Amazon's strict SLA.
- **Shipped COGS** – This metric is based on the cost price of a product at the time of Amazon purchasing it, multiplied by the shipped volume during the selected time period. Expressed as a dollar value and calculated as: Vendor Cost Price * Volume Shipped (to end customers). Shipped COGS equals Amazon PCOGs.
- **Shipped Revenue** – The revenue Amazon makes by shipping a vendor's products. It's based on the average selling price to the end customer at the time of shipment and multiplied by the sold volume during the selected time period. Calculated as: ASP * Volume Shipped (to end customers).
- **Shipped Volume** – Equals shipped revenue ÷ ASP.
- **SIA** – Sell-in agreement. Margin funding for Amazon that is granted as a percentage or $ amount per shipped item to Amazon warehouses.
- **SIOC** – Ships in Own Container. Describes products that don't need an Amazon overbox.

- **SKU** – Stock Keeping Unit. A unique code to identify a product.
- **SLA** – Service Level Agreement
- **SnS** – Subscribe and Save. Amazon's loyalty programme to entice customers to make repeat purchases of replenishable products on its marketplace in exchange for a small discount.
- **SnL** – Small and Light. Fulfilment programme that results in low shipping costs for qualified products that fit into an envelope.
- **SOA** – Sell-out Agreement. Margin funding for Amazon that is granted as a percentage or $ amount per sold item to end customers.
- **SoROOS** – Sourceable Replenishment Out of Stock. This metric measures the instances when products are shown as unavailable for purchase on the product detail page, even though they can be sourced from a 1P vendor. Factors that affect SoROOS include temporary sales suppression due to repeat customer complaints or safety concerns (Andon Cords), manual buyer suppressions, and lack of inventory.
- **SP-API** – Selling Partner API. A suite of REST-based APIs that provides Amazon selling partners programmatic access to their Amazon Seller or Vendor Central account data.
- **SPN** – Service Provider Network
- **SR** – Sales Rank. The ranking of an item in a product category.
- **SRP** – Secure Receive Process

- **SRP** – Suggested Retail Price
- **SSCC** – Serial Shipping Container Code. External Container ID to label cartons to be sent to Amazon, which can be passed via Electronic Data Interchange (EDI).
- **STR** – Sell-Through Rate. Calculated as the number of units shipped compared to the number of units at Amazon at the start of the period, plus any units received during the same time period. Sell Through Rate = (Shipped units – customer returns) / (On hand units + received units).
- **Storefront** – A curated brand store, typically paid for by vendors.
- **SW** – Ship Window. The date range in which a PO needs to be delivered to an Amazon warehouse to avoid chargebacks.
- **T5** – Turkey Five. Refers to the five days stretching from Thanksgiving to Cyber Monday, otherwise known as Thanksgiving weekend.
- **T12M** – Trailing 12 Months
- **Third-Party Seller** – Describes sellers trading goods on Amazon's marketplace without selling these items to Amazon first.
- **TL** – Truck Load
- **TOS** – Terms of Service
- **TTM** – Trailing Twelve Months
- **UFT** – Ultra Fast Track (UFT). The percentage of time that an ASIN can be shipped to the customer from a fulfilment centre, versus the selection Amazon intended to carry.

- **UNSPSC** – United Nations Standard Product and Services Code. Amazon uses this code to categorise products.
- **UPC** – Universal Product Code. 12 numeric digits that are uniquely assigned to a product item for tracking it in-store.
- **UX** –User Experience
- **Variation** – Products available in different colours, sizes, and forms, grouped on a detail page.
- **VAT** – Value Added Tax
- **VC** – Vendor Central. The admin interface used by manufacturers and distributors who work directly with Amazon as a first-party vendor (1P).
- **VCR** – Vendor Confirmation Rate
- **Vendor** – Describes brands that sell directly to Amazon instead of to end customers. Amazon places the orders and takes care of pricing and inventory management.
- **VF / Vflex** – Vendor Flex. A supply chain programme through which vendors supply products to end customers out of their warehouse.
- **VVF** – Virtual Vendor Flex. Like Vendor Flex, but the vendor, not Amazon, provides the labor for picking and packing the shipments to the end customer.
- **VFMC** – Vendor Funded Managed Coupons. Set up and managed by Amazon's Subscribe and Save team.

- **Vine** – An Amazon program where sellers can register their products to receive reviews from verified product testers.
- **VIP** – Vendor Improvement Plan. Outlines the metrics that the AVS Brand Specialist is targeting to improve with a vendor.
- **VIR** – Volume Incentive Rates. Refers to rebates that are granted either as a fixed or tiered percentage. They incentivize Amazon to buy additional volume from vendors.
- **VLT** – Vendor Lead Time
- **Voucher (also: Vendor Powered Voucher, or VPV)** – A type of discount vendors and sellers can offer to customers. Customers redeem the vouchers on the product detail page.
- **Warehouse Deal** – Used or returned items sold at a discount to Amazon customers to prevent waste and reduce the liquidation of imperfect products.
- **WCO** – World Customs Organisation
- **WEEE** – Waste Electronic and Electrical Equipment
- **WOC** – Weeks of Cover. A metric used to measure how many weeks of demand Amazon currently holds in inventory for a product.
- **WoW** – Week over Week
- **X-Channel Management** – Refers to brands selling their products across multiple Amazon channels (e.g., Amazon Core, Fresh, Go, etc.).

- **YTD** – Year to Date
  YoY – Year over Year
- **Zero Inventories** – Refers to an inventory control mechanism that eliminates any waste due to built-up inventory levels. Sellers stock only the items they need and intend to sell within a certain time period.

NOTE

It's essential to stay informed about Amazon's policies and guidelines related to customer communication, marketing, and promotions as they may evolve over time. Always ensure that your strategies align with Amazon's terms of service. For the most current and accurate information, refer to Amazon's official documentation and seller guidelines.

DISCLAIMER:

This book refers to the term "Amazon" for training & education purposes only. The use of the name "Amazon" is not intended to claim any ownership, affiliation, or endorsement by Amazon or its parent company, Amazon.com the Amazon name mentioned in this book is the exclusive property of Amazon.com. All rights to the Amazon name, logo, and trademark are acknowledged and belong solely to Amazon.com.

This book is not authorized, endorsed, or affiliated with Amazon or Amazon.com. It is designed for educational and training purposes only. Any references made to Amazon are used descriptively and are not intended to infringe upon the intellectual property rights of Amazon.com.

www.ingramcontent.com/pod-product-compliance
Lightning Source LLC
Chambersburg PA
CBHW071109240526
45469CB00006BD/2398